A FAMILY SECRET

A graphic novel of courage and resistance
brought to you by the Anne Frank House

Eric Heuvel

A FAMILY SECRET

A graphic novel of courage and resistance
brought to you by the Anne Frank House

MACMILLAN CHILDREN'S BOOKS

Helena's parents,
Mr. and Mrs. Van Dort

Helena and her two brothers,
Wim and Theo

Dr. and Mrs. Hecht and Esther

Helena and her grandson, Jeroen

Esther

Each year on April 30,
a myriad of activities take place in the Netherlands
to celebrate Dutch Queen's Day.
All over the country, people go out into the streets.
There is live music everywhere, lots of good food and drink,
and secondhand things are bought and sold.
Jeroen decides to go over to his grandmother's house to see
if she has anything he can sell.

Jeroen only has a few days left to gather up some old things for the Queen's Day flea market.

Maybe I should have called first.

There's gotta be great stuff at Gran's!

Jeroen, sweet boy! Here to see your old granny again?

Yes, Gran... but I also need a favor...

64

So you want to poke around in my attic for things to sell at the flea market?

Please!

Hmm... All right, but let's have a cup of tea first.

I've already found lots of old things in our attic, but I bet there's some good things here as well.

Show me what you plan to take with you, okay?

Is there lots of stuff up there?

Yes, your grandpa saved everything... I haven't been in the attic for years...

What a mess!

A cloth star... ...Jew? Strange...

The 1936 Olympic Games in Berlin! Wow, that was a long time ago!

3 gold medals! Why wouldn't Hitler shake his hand?

JESSE OWENS WINT 3e GOUD

HITLER WEIGE[RT] ZWARTE ATLE[ET] TE FELICITERE[N]

I wonder who made this?

DUITSCHE JEUGD IN DEN HITLER-JUGEND

JOODSCHE V[LU]CHTEN WIJKEN UIT N[AAR]

DUITSCH LEGER STEEDS STERKER

Jeroen is not aware of how much time has passed...

Rusland v[alt] Finland binnen

HITLER IN PRAAG!

VREDE IN ONZE TIJD!

Duitschland één grote kazerne

Vervolging Joden in Duitschland verscherpt

Burgeroorlog in Spanje

Japan neemt Nanking in

Akkoord te München

Crisis om Sudetenland

Articles from before World War II.

Maybe there's a name somewhere...

Helena? That's Gran! So this belongs to her...

Helena & Esther 1939

Jeroen! Are you still alive? You're awfully quiet!

Uh... yeah... Everything's fine. Hey, Gran! I found your old scrapbook!

Isn't this yours?

Gran, aren't you happy that I found it?

Oh, dear... It was so long ago...

I'll tell you why I started this scrapbook.

Okay...

Let's hope this doesn't take long!

It's very hard to talk about what happened... Such a dreadful time, so we never discussed it in our family... It's a family secret...

I was 12 when I started it. That was in 1938. I kept track of the news. My older brothers thought I was a bookworm. They were always fighting with each other.

The German Chancellor, Hitler, is being welcomed by an enthusiastic crowd.

You're a cheater!

I don't wanna play anymore!

Theo, Wim, stop arguing!

A person can't even hear the news.

My father was a policeman and we lived in Amsterdam.

What's for dinner? I'm starved!

Meat loaf, potatoes...

So you're the one with blond hair, but who's this pretty girl?

Helena & Esther 1939

Sigh... Esther...

Esther was my best friend. She was originally from Germany...

It's as if it were yesterday... Esther coming to live in our apartment building. But it was the winter of 1938.

Our downstairs neighbors had already heard who was going to live in the empty apartment...

It seems they're Jews from Germany...

How can that be... I thought they closed the Dutch borders to refugees in May?

I was very curious about our new neighbors...

Do you see a removals truck?

No, just a car...

Actually, the people in that car were our new neighbors.

Your new home is up there in that building...

The apartment is a bit small, but with such short notice, it was difficult to find anything else, Dr. Hecht...

It will do just fine...

Hi there, I'm Helena!

Ich heisse Esther...

I was glad Esther was placed in my class at school.

Boys and girls, this is Esther. She's from Karlsruhe in Germany. Do your best to make her feel at home.

tien daagse veldtocht → 18:

1870 Franse oor

We worked on Esther's Dutch every day on our way home from school.

When you can pronounce the city of "Scheveningen" in Dutch, then you've got it...

Skev, Schefe...ening, eh.

Not everyone was happy about the new neighbors.

What are all these foreigners doing here?

So many people are already out of work!

In no time, Esther could speak Dutch. She began to tell me stories about Germany... dreadful stories.

We had to flee... I had to leave all my things in Germany. I could only take some clothes...

Was it that bad?

Yes. It all started in 1933, when Hitler's party came to power.

Once we get rid of Germany's Jews, there'll be no more poverty and unemployment!

Heil Hitler! All right!

One of the first things Hitler did was abolish all other political parties. He was like a dictator from then on.

If you're not with us, you're against us! And you'll feel our wrath!

Hitler had gangs of thugs—the SA.* Lots of his opponents were beaten up and many were imprisoned in concentration camps.

Now we're in charge!

I'll teach you, you filthy socialist!

From now on, might is right!

*Storm Troopers

There was some resistance. Our neighbor who spoke out against the Nazis was arrested... a very nice man.

They're taking him to a concentration camp!

Shhh...

What an outrage!

He should have kept his mouth shut!

Jews were also affected. My father is a doctor, but all of a sudden he was only allowed to treat Jewish patients. The Nazis hung a sign on his office door as a warning to non-Jews.

Nobody will dare visit this Jew doctor now!

Good, he'll go bankrupt!

Dr. med. M. Hecht

Achtung Jude!
Besuch
verboten

I'm still not changing doctors!

More and more Germans supported Hitler. Unemployment and poverty had decreased because Hitler was building a powerful army.

Germany isn't big enough for us. We must have more land!

I will make Germany a mighty nation again!

New factories and highways were constructed...

A prosperous new Germany...

These new roads are going to come in handy!

Reichs-autobahn
Nürnberg
München

Juden unerwünscht

Konditorei

"Jews Not Welcome." What do they have against us?

Teachers who disagreed with the Nazis were fired. Children were taught to hate Jews.

I repeat the words of our leader Adolf Hitler: The Jew is our greatest enemy.

Der Jude ist unser grözter Feind! Hütet euch vor dem Juden

There were kids who wanted to beat me up after school, so when the bell rang I ran home as fast as I could.

Filthy Jew!

Things got much worse...

A Jewish youngster has murdered a German diplomat...

Hmm, a perfect excuse to teach all the Jews in Germany a lesson!

We'll "arrange" for the masses to rise up in anger!

On the night of November 9, 1938, gangs of Nazi thugs turned out all over Germany...

There's also a Jewish shop down there!

No, to the synagogue first!

Hit 'em where it hurts!

Our synagogue went up in flames...

Where are the fire trucks?

They're not coming. Isn't that obvious?

The clothing store across the street was destroyed...

Why isn't any-one stopping this?

They've gone too far now.

This was later called Kristallnacht, or the "Night of Broken Glass." Hundreds of synagogues and thousands of shops were also destroyed. My uncle was imprisoned in a concentration camp, just like 30,000 other German Jews.

We were scared to death. What could we do?

Flee? Where to? So many countries in Europe have closed their borders.

We've booked passage on a ship sailing for Argentina. If I were you, I wouldn't wait much longer.

13

My father called a colleague in Holland who agreed to help us...

Are you really sure this is a good idea?

Of course! Once Hitler is gone we'll just go home.

KARLSRUHE ARNHEIM

Not everybody could get into the Netherlands...

You're only welcome here if you have enough money...

I used to have enough, but I had to leave it behind!

Go home, then!

But we were fortunate.

Here's our invitation from Professor Bouwer... He's picking us up.

Yes, there's a man waiting for you!

UITGANG PERRON 1

And that's how we arrived in Amsterdam with just a few suitcases.

The worst is over, Dr. Hecht. I'm busy arranging a job for you at the hospital where I work...

So what happened finally? Did Esther ever return to Germany?

No, because the war began here...

Newsreel footage of Hitler was now shown in our movie theaters, and everywhere, even in Holland, Nazism grew...

All people who speak German should live in one country. Germans are superior—the strongest and smartest people in the world.

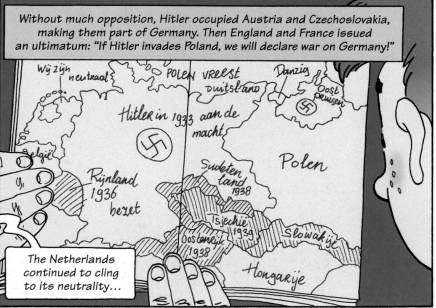

Without much opposition, Hitler occupied Austria and Czechoslovakia, making them part of Germany. Then England and France issued an ultimatum: "If Hitler invades Poland, we will declare war on Germany!"

The Netherlands continued to cling to its neutrality...

On September 1, 1939, the powerful German Army invaded Poland...

England reacted immediately.

...consequently this country is at war with Germany.

But nobody helped the Polish Army, and they didn't have a chance.

Attack!

This is pointless!

They're too strong.

The radio spoke of atrocities committed against the Poles.

Ready, aim, FIRE...

After Poland's defeat, things were quiet for a while...

Let's hope the worst is over now.

Oh, we don't need to worry about anything. After all, Holland is neutral...

Yet I really admire the German Army. It's so modern and efficient.

Why don't you shut up, Theo!

Then in the spring of 1940, the German Army occupied Norway and Denmark.

Our neutrality has gone too far... pretending to defend ourselves against England!

While everybody knows Germany is the real threat!

The Dutch Army was poorly equipped.

Think we can hit anything with this 1896 canon?

I think the rifle I'm using is even older.

We might have had half a chance—against the Romans!

May 10, 1940. I was awakened by the noise of airplanes.

They're going to bomb the airport outside the city!

War, we're at war!

What will my family do now?

We were all glued to the news!

Shh, the Queen.

People of the Netherlands, last night, without the slightest provocation, the German Army launched a surprise attack on our territory...

The German Army is falling from the sky!

So much for defending our nation!

Let's hope they all drown in the sea...

The radio reported heavy fighting at the Afsluitdijk, the strategic dam in the north of the country.

The Dutch are too entrenched!

Their bunkers are too strong!

The Dutch troops put up a brave fight...

They don't call us the elite German forces for nothing. This will be over in no time!

Those were such nerve-wracking days... so much confusion...

The newspaper says the German Army has experienced a setback.

It's a bunch of propaganda. We're powerless against the German Army.

It seems thousands are already dead...

The Dutch Queen fled to England.

That's good news because now the Krauts* won't capture her.

What a coward. She's abandoned us.

Non-sense!

*Offensive slang for Germans

The war reached our doorstep...

Oh my goodness, they're bombing Amsterdam!

They've hit the oil tanks in the harbor!

Now we're doomed...

Esther and her parents tried to flee again...

Why are you leaving?

We're going to try to find a ship that's sailing for England...

But they couldn't escape... The roads were blocked...

Go back!

IJmuiden

Amsterdam

Please let us through, we're Jews... Our lives are in danger!

The advance was taking too long for Germany's generals...

We're behind schedule. This battle in the Netherlands has already taken 4 days!

We'll issue an ultimatum: we'll bomb Rotterdam if they don't capitulate!

While negotiations about the surrender were under way, on May 14, German bombers took off...

This'll be a cinch! Rotterdam doesn't have any anti-aircraft defenses.

The bombers appeared above the center of the city...

What's going on? The ultimatum doesn't expire for three hours!

Oh no! What a disaster!

Stay in formation, carpet the city with bombs... open hatch doors... BOMBS AWAY!!!

That's how the old center of Rotterdam was destroyed...

The Germans also threatened to bomb the city of Utrecht...

Countrymen... Today, May 14... the Dutch Army has agreed to lay down its weapons...

17

The next day, the German Army rolled into Amsterdam...

Where are we going?

To see the Germans... It was on the radio.

There's so many of them!

Now we're in trouble...

The Dutch Nazis were happy about the Occupation...

Welcome to Amsterdam!

Now we're in charge!

We're gonna put things right. Finally!

Look, Helena! Your father is directing traffic with that German soldier!

Yes. He's on duty today.

Yesterday we were fighting them, today we're collaborating...

Much to our surprise, the German soldiers were well-behaved.

Very nice boys, they bought up all my chocolate. Didn't steal a thing, simply paid for it all!

Later...

Uh-oh. What's that hearse doing on our street?

Your mother is crying.

Mother! What happened?

The old Jewish couple from No. 60... committed suicide!

They were so afraid of the future...

The German Occupier quickly disbanded the parliament.

Yes, that was to be expected. Now we really won't have a say.

Wow, this German Army is invincible. Nobody's capable of defeating them!

The newspapers only report what the Germans permit.

...With the defeat of the Netherlands, Belgium and France, the battle now turns to England.

July 1940.

Corrie, I'm a police officer... I can't break the law. I don't want anyone in this house listening to the BBC!!!

You can't be serious?!? How will we get any accurate news about the war? The Krauts only broadcast their lies to us.

Certain items such as coffee, tea and soap became scarce. People received monthly ration coupons. You needed these coupons to purchase goods.

My mother wants to know if we can get a bit more soap?

No. There's a soap shortage and it's divided as fairly as possible. Your coupon, please.

Autumn arrived...

What's wrong, Esther?

...sob... At the market-place, Dutch Nazis were fighting with the Jewish merchants!

Don't get so upset. The police will make sure this doesn't happen again.

No, this is exactly how it began in Germany...

My brothers continued fighting with each other...

What discipline! The Dutch can learn a lot from these Germans!

Nonsense, Theo. Have you forgotten what they're doing in Poland? Wait till you really get to know them...

A while later...

How come you know about Poland, Wim?

You didn't really think I would obey Father? I listen to the BBC in secret whenever I can...

My father was frequently in a bad mood. There were lots of changes at the police department.

Believe me, Corrie, to advance my career, I have to join the Dutch Nazi Party. Only party members will be promoted.

Have you completely lost your mind?

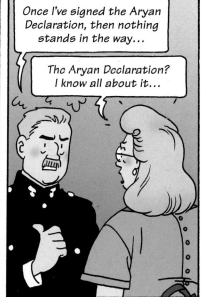

Once I've signed the Aryan Declaration, then nothing stands in the way...

The Aryan Declaration? I know all about it...

19

A declaration telling the Nazis exactly who's Jewish and who isn't can only mean trouble!

Woman, you worry too much...

These days it's every man for himself...

It was the WA (Storm Troopers from the Dutch Nazi Party) who especially terrorized the Jews.

WA, keep marching. Marching for our people and our fatherland!

What is it, old man—don't like our song? Then you must be a Jew!

Let's end ritual slaughter once and for all. This Jewish butcher shop is closed now!

The Germans are here, so now the scum dare...

Some Jewish men fought back.

Just hang on to me, you'll be okay.

Good riddance to bad rubbish!

In February 1941, a Dutch Nazi was killed. The German Occupier was furious and, as revenge, 427 Jews were rounded up. Almost all of them were sent to Mauthausen concentration camp in Austria, a certain death...

Many Amsterdamers went on strike in protest, including city employees. The streetcars did not operate.

Come join us, man!

Too dangerous for me...

But what's being done to Jews is appalling!!

The Germans were completely surprised. This hadn't happened in other countries they'd occupied!

STRIKE, STRIKE, STRIKE!

They're also striking in towns outside Amsterdam!

Troublemakers! Let's beat them to a pulp...

C'mon... calm down. These are our fellow countrymen...

It isn't pretty, but we have to follow orders!

The police cleared the main square downtown of protesters... as well as the rest of Amsterdam.

Go inside! Or we'll open fire!

Hey, don't shoot at your own people!

They'd shoot their own mothers if ordered to do so.

The next day they did open fire on the crowd. The strike ended quickly... The streetcars started running again, each with a policeman aboard.

All the city employees have gone back to work. I don't need a bullet in my head.

They're still striking in the outskirts of the city... It's dangerous.

The Germans arrested many protesters.

Has the strike now ended?

Yes, it's pointless for people to resist...

March 1941. For almost a year, the Nazis had tried to convince the entire Dutch population to join them. But they had not succeeded.

The Dutch must now choose for National Socialism. You're either with us or against us! We will deal harshly with those who resist!

To prove they meant business, the Germans executed three strikers and fifteen members of one Resistance group.

C'mon, you're next in line...

Still, more people, Jews and non-Jews, joined the Resistance. For example, illegal newspapers were distributed.

A few classmates and I have an underground school newspaper.

Be careful, Wim! You can be arrested for that...

In April, everyone was issued an identity card, a sort of passport.

Take your identity card with you, Corrie!

Ration coupons, identity cards... what will they think up next?!

But we were doing a lot better than Esther and her parents...

What's with your father? He didn't even say hello!

He isn't allowed to work at the hospital anymore. Jewish doctors are only allowed to treat Jewish patients.

Jews were isolated step by step. One warm day we wanted to go to the swimming pool...

No Jews Allowed?!

Then I won't go swimming either!

VERBODEN VOOR JODEN

ZWEMBAD

My family was always arguing.

Now, you listen to me, young man...

...the spertijd* also applies to you. You'd better be home on time tonight!

Just because you play policeman out there, doesn't mean you get to be one here too!

*Curfew requiring people to leave the streets and be home at a prescribed hour

All your rules make me crazy...

Things were bad at home.

This is the last time I'm going to warn you, boy!

I'll do what I want!

...to preserve Western civilization... We're fighting the barbarians from the East...

Father! Theo! Hitler has attacked Russia!

We are faithful to our leader Adolf Hitler...

...From Finland to the Black Sea, the German Army is advancing, supported by Finnish, Italian, Romanian and Hungarian comrades.

The following day the papers were filled with news.

Russia is a goner!

?!

I'm going to Esther's...

What a great adventure!

23 JUNI 1941

Proclamatie van Hitler aan Duitsche volk

Rusland

Groot-Duitsche Rijk

Gevechten aan de geheele Russische grens gisteren begonnen.

Wat doet Nederland

ACTIE IN HET OOSTEN WOR STELSELMATIG VOORTGE

I feel much more at home at their place.

Hi, Mrs. Hecht. Is Esther around?

Come in. Esther has gotten some bad news...

I can't go back to our school after summer. Jewish students have to go to separate schools.

That's terrible!

We can't do anything about it... But the new school is close to our school...

At least we'll still be able to walk to school together!

It was more enjoyable to be at Esther's, but her family also had their worries.

I already said it in 1938! We should have gone to America.

How could we have known the Nazis would occupy the Netherlands?

I'm so glad we can go back to school...

Me too. I get crazy at home...

V = Victorie
Duitschland wint op alle fronten

I'll see you right after school!

My history teacher at school was replaced by a member of the Dutch Nazi Party. We immediately hated him.

...and in this book, Hitler explained his ideas. He already wrote in 1925 that...

Leningrad

Moskou

De strijd tegen het communisme is een strijd om te overleven

Krim

Why is Esther so late?

Esther! What happened?

...There were boys waiting for us after school... They called us names and hurled a stone through a classroom window...

Cowards!

Perhaps my father can do something about it...

How can you enforce all these German regulations?

Wim, I have to. They're in charge.

I have no time to talk about this... Duty calls.

Father! You have to help Esther!

Help? What's wrong?

Esther and her classmates are being harassed by some bullies. Isn't there something you can do?

Don't blow it all out of proportion...

Helena, Jews shouldn't expect any protection from the police. I don't understand why Father is still a policeman...

What other choices does he have? Resigning? How would we get by?

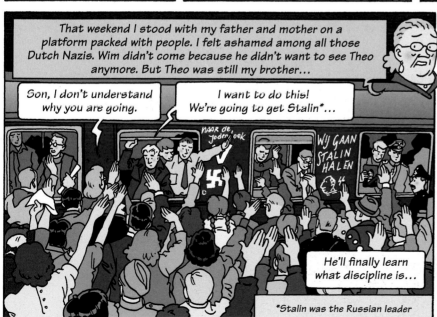

Just a few weeks later, a letter arrived from Theo:

...I'm now at basic training...

Men, you will soon become part of the brotherhood defending the Greater German Reich...

...it is very hard, but we're learning a lot...

I want to hear those boots, you bunch of weaklings! We're going to make you real soldiers!

...and my closet has never been so orderly...

Your closet is a mess! Take your neighbor as an example. Your leave is cancelled!

...and if we go to the fairgrounds, I'll do great at the shooting gallery.

Very good shot! That's what we need!

...We're also taught about Adolf Hitler's ideology.

Our greatest enemies are the Jews and the Russians. It is a battle about life or death!

STRIJDT MEE !

...Taking the oath of allegiance was a very solemn moment...

We swear our loyalty to Adolf Hitler, Führer of the Greater German Reich.

Then a note arrived that Theo was being sent to the front...

Oh, how awful! We'll probably never see him again!

Stop sniveling. He'll be fine!

Gébé
EI-SURROGAAT

A month later, another letter arrived from Theo:

I'm now at the front...

Where are they getting all these Russian soldiers? Everyone said Russia was almost defeated!

Yeah, almost...

While the combat in Russia dragged on, in December 1941, Japan launched a surprise attack on the American fleet at Pearl Harbor...

And now what?!

Japan was an ally of Hitler's Germany.

...and that's why our Führer Adolf Hitler has now declared war on the United States...

Now the whole world is at war!

...our trusted ally Japan will drive the Americans, the British and the Dutch out of Asia...

Oh, how terrible! I hope nothing bad happens to Aunt Riek...

Aunt Riek was my mother's sister. In 1935, she'd moved to the Dutch East Indies with her husband and son. It's now called Indonesia...

Is that big dagger from there?

Yes, it's called a Javanese kris.

My Aunt Riek lived on Java, one of the islands in the Dutch East Indies. I always dreamed about visiting her.

Nederlandsch Oost-Indië vergeleken met Europa

Schoolplaat XIV

If you compare the size of our colony to Europe...

Japan had been preparing for this war for years.

We want to rule Asia the same way that Germany rules Europe.

Asia for the Asians! Westerners, go home!

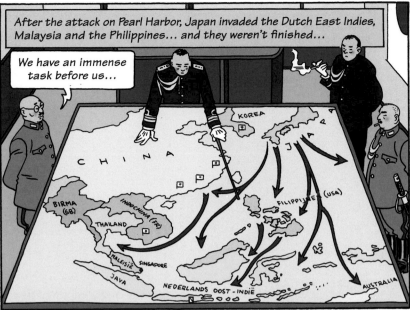

After the attack on Pearl Harbor, Japan invaded the Dutch East Indies, Malaysia and the Philippines... and they weren't finished...

We have an immense task before us...

A naval fleet of American, British and Dutch ships went down fighting...

The enemy has been defeated...

Tomorrow we will take the island of Java!

Many natives of the Dutch East Indies hoped Japan would free them from Dutch dominance.

The Japanese will help us gain independence!

TOKO MAKASSAR

MODE

I'm afraid they're going to be our new oppressor...

Aunt Riek was there when the Japanese Army landed...

Belandas,* go home!

What will happen now?

*Dutch

Many Europeans were imprisoned in Japanese camps, including Aunt Riek, Uncle Cor, and their son, André.

You have 15 minutes to pack what you can carry. You're going to a work camp and your property will be confiscated!

After the war, we finally heard what had happened to them. They went through terrible times...

Gran, that dagger, uh... the kris...

It's yours if you want it...

...But during that time I didn't think about the Dutch East Indies much!

Het Joodsche Weekblad

Discrimination against Jews increased...

There are so many restrictions...

...No biking, driving, going to the zoo. We're not allowed in the library...

...We can no longer belong to a sports club...

We're not even allowed to sit in this small park anymore... Everything's forbidden!

Voor Joden verboden

Wim joined the Resistance...

I'll distribute them this week...

Be careful, all right?

Printing and distributing underground newspapers was punishable by death.

Father mustn't find out...

HET PAROOL
VRIJ ONVERVEERD

I secretly passed copies to all our neighbors.

There's an article on doctors and the Resistance.

Hi, may I come in? What's wrong?

VERDUISTERD
BESCHERMD

Esther really needs you now...

Esther!

Oh no! Huh? What's the meaning of this?

Those evil monsters! Now they can easily see who's Jewish. It's so degrading!

I couldn't do anything to help... Jews even had to pay for the stars themselves! This is the one Esther gave me...

What if you just didn't sew it on your clothes?

Jood

The punishment was severe. You also always had to have your identity card with you. This was mine, but there was a capital J on the identity cards of Jews!

It was spring and beautiful weather, but things at home were still bad.

What were you thinking, bringing these underground newspapers here?!

Don't do that! I have to distribute those papers!

You will not! It's forbidden and now it's over! Say goodbye to this junk!

You will stop this immediately! You're putting our lives at risk!

I won't stop... It's much too important.

When Father was out, we listened to Radio Orange, the Dutch station broadcasting from London.

...So be it then, we'll get the latest news this way!

This is Radio Orange, the voice of fighting Holland...

...The Germans have not managed to reconquer the area around Moscow.

Yes! For the first time the German Army has been stopped!

But what about Theo?

A few weeks later we heard from Theo.

I was wounded during a bombardment, but was very lucky. I'm up for some leave and I'll come home to recover in the hospital there...

Mother and I went to visit him in the hospital.

I'm so happy to see you. I'm already feeling much better.

We fought hard against the Russians, but the winter was unbearable.

We don't even have decent winter jackets.

The Russians are used to this dreadful cold!

We thought it'd be an easy victory, but the Russian Army was very determined...

Luckily, the winter is almost over...

We were attacked at the beginning of April...

TAKE COVER!!! AIR RAID!

ARGH!!

My friend Karel is dead. Many comrades gave up their lives for the cause. Yet sometimes I really wonder...

What?

Awful things happen in wartime...

??

One day we were in a village behind the front lines...

What kind of soldiers are those? Never seen them on the front!

Where are they taking those civilians?

Those are death squads... for special missions.

Civilians? Those are Jews, man.

Special missions? What kind of special mis—

RATATATATATATAT

—sions?

It can't be true!

I don't want you to go back, Theo!

But I have to! We will win this war...

You'll be careful, my boy?

Say hello to Father...

That was the last time I saw Theo. One afternoon a letter arrived...

Mother! What's wrong?

...killed in action for Führer, Folk and Fatherland...

My mother was terribly upset... but my father scarcely reacted...

My mother tried talking to him about it.

Are you listening to me?!?

Not another word about Theo!

My parents argued all the time.

I'm not blind. Don't you think I see how the police collaborate with the Germans...

You'll have dirty hands!

What do you want? That I resign, be sent off to Germany?

Maybe that would be better...

What nonsense!

Are you going out? Can I come? They're driving me crazy!

No, you can't come.

Then I'll go out alone!

Why are you outside? It's going to rain!

Much better than being inside!

Father, I'll stay with Helena until the storm is over. It's so muggy!

See you later!

My father and I heard horrible rumors this afternoon—

Hey, look who's here!

Don't let it bother you... There are other boys!!!

Oh, you're both soaked...

Wait, I'll get you some towels.

What did you mean by "horrible rumors"?

They say all the Jews are going to be sent to Germany to work in labor camps for the Nazis...

Again, it's only rumors...

However, this rumor was true. One summer day in 1942, Esther was very upset after school.

A few students have received a call-up. They've been ordered to report!

Postmen brought the call-up notices door-to-door. Later the police had to do it.

Is your son at home?

In the weeks following, more and more Jews received these notices...

You must report. What choice is there?

Just don't go...

But then the police come to get you...

Many Jews who chose to ignore these orders were rounded up.

Handy that we know exactly where the Jews live...

Outside... right now!

We can't go yet, our daughter is still at school...

We'll pick her up too...

The Nazis organized razzias: they would close off a street or a neighborhood and search all the houses. One day there was a roundup near my school.

All Jews must leave their homes right now. Bring only one suitcase along with you!

Your identity card...

Teachers from Esther's school were taken too...

Mr. De Winter will not be returning. French class is now cancelled...

§12 → 5 t/m 12

J'habite un
Dans la ma

Her classmates disappeared without warning...

Martin and Tineke are gone...

Let's hope they went into hiding...

It's difficult to go into hiding... You need money and the help of non-Jewish friends...

And it's dangerous. If you're caught...

We're going to try anyway...

There were more and more razzias in Amsterdam. Many Jews were rounded up and registered...

...They were taken by streetcar to the train station.

Last year the conductors went out on strike...

Now they're simply too afraid to help us...

I'm happy we're not Jews.

Afterwards, they were sent to Westerbork Transit Camp in the northeast of the Netherlands.

Anyone who disobeys our rules will immediately be transported to the East!

Trains left weekly from Westerbork carrying men, women and children to unknown destinations in eastern Europe.

I hope we'll be reunited with our parents...

Quiet over there! Move along!

They treat us like we're cattle...

We'll probably be picked up soon as well.

Can't you go somewhere?

BEPERKTE BEWEGINGSVRIJHEID VOOR JODEN

Possibly... My father is trying to arrange a hiding place for us.

Esther and her parents were running out of time...

When are you all going into hiding?

It's almost arranged...

Here, this necklace is for you. As a token of our close friendship. This might be the last time we see each other...

They were too late. One morning in September 1942...

Having to do this in your own neighborhood...

I hear you. I couldn't get reassigned...

Jews live in that building. Make sure nobody escapes.

Meijer family! Downstairs right now!

My mother was shocked when she saw that my father had been assigned to that razzia...

Oh no! He said only Dutch Nazis working for the police did these roundups.

Waaah... Mommy!

Keep moving!

But... wait, that's Helena's father!

Can't you please help us?

...Esther... She's still at school. Please warn her and tell her where they're taking us...

Uh... I don't... I'll see what I can do...

Faster! Faster!

I... Wait... OUCH!

Uh... um, uh, easy on these people. They're not resisting...

I'll wait here for Esther. Then you can travel together!

When the razzia was over, my father lingered behind.

Too many Jewish children are getting away...

I'll pick her up and then report in...

It's best if I wait in here for Esther to return...

What are you doing here in the Hechts' apartment? What's going on?

I promised that I would bring Esther to join her parents...

Father! How can you help the Germans?

If I don't, they'd just fire me on the spot! Don't think I'm happy about this, but...

Now you've gone too far!

Just shut up! I've heard enough. I'm going to get Esther!

It was late when my father got home. I had stayed up until he returned.

There he is! Alone!

Father, what happened? Where's Esther?

I did what I had to do. Discussion closed!

What my father did then... I never forgave him for it. Look, this is the necklace that Esther gave me. I wear it all the time.

My life was changed forever. I missed my best friend so much. Everything I saw around me reminded me of her...

Oh, they're emptying out more Jewish homes.

Like they did with the Hechts'... Oh, Esther...

What do you do with all these things?

They go to people in Germany who've been hit by the Allied bombings.

I can't stand being at home, Wim. Can't I help you with the newspaper runs?

It's too dangerous...

I know, but I still want to do it...

I'll talk to my friends about it. It's true, a girl attracts less attention...

There's something I have to do. Go straight home.

We all have our secrets. Wim in the Resistance... Father and his work...

We had less and less contact with Father.

You use our home like it's a hotel...

39

Fine! Go and hide at work! I'm surprised you're not working even more overtime.

Grumble...

The weeks passed...

I'm going to get some air. I still have ration coupons for meat. Maybe there is some... You'll stay here?

Sigh... Yes, Mother.

Later...

Hey, sis. Is the old man still at work?

Yes, and Mom's asleep. She waited in line for meat for hours.

Your attention for an extra bulletin from the headquarters of the Führer...

...in Russia... Heroic until the last man and bullet, the German Sixth Army has been defeated at Stalingrad.

Did you hear that?

The German Army's been hit hard!

BRRRRrrrrrrrooooaaaa

Listen! British planes...

I'll turn off the lights so we can see! Pull back the blackout curtains!

...a period of mourning has been declared in the entire Reich, but...

They're headed for Germany!

Germany is being attacked from all sides. The war is almost over...

We read in the newspapers that German cities were bombed. But many Allied planes were shot down en route to Germany.

I've lost control! We're going down!

Where are we?

I'm not really sure!

Some pilots managed to parachute from their planes in time. The Resistance quite often found them a hiding place...

Speak up! Any sign of the crew?

I saw somebody on the road...

Don't know...

Via Radio Orange broadcasts, we heard that the German Army in Russia had to keep on retreating...

So it was sink or swim for them...

Exactly! In Berlin, Minister of Public Enlightenment and Propaganda Goebbels incited the German people to fight to the bitter end.

The English say that you're tired of war... that's why I'm asking you...

...DO YOU WANT TOTAL WAR?!?

TOTALER KRIEG - KÜRZESTER KRIEG

YESSSSS!!!

Many German men were called up for the army. The Dutch military, captured in May 1940 and later released, was ordered to go and work in Germany. People really resented this.

Naturally, our soldiers don't want to go to Germany to work. This calls for a strike!

Is striking a good idea?

NEDERLANDERS STAAKT! ALGEMENE STAKING

At the end of April 1943, strikes began all over Holland.

BEKENDMAKING

Demonstrators must be shot...

The first protesters were executed right away...

That should scare them off...

Nobody will dare strike now!

The strike was over within a matter of days...

It's an uneven fight...

That won't stop us...

Resistance increased...

What's happening here is a disgrace!

We can't just sit here!

You're right!

There was an armed resistance...

He deserved it! Now he can't betray any more Resistance people!

Let's go!

There was sabotage...

So now the Krauts can use carrier pigeons...

Resistance groups became much better organized.

We're preparing a vital operation. Can you help us get some German Army uniforms?

We need ten false identity cards...

Now not only Jews, but Resistance fighters also had to go into hiding. The LO was a nationwide network that helped these people by arranging hiding places for them...

You're already the fifth this week...

Our Resistance group was betrayed.

When Wim turned 18, he received a call-up...

I have to go and work in Germany!

You're not going to do that?!

No, I'll go into hiding now. You'll tell Mother?

Of course!

I'll miss him so...

The LO arranged for Wim to hide at a farm in the east of the Netherlands.

You're not our only guest...

Thanks! If I can ever help you in return...

Welcome, son. You'll have to share the hayloft with a few other people...

No problem!

Wim was given a false identity card and started working with the local Resistance...

Wim de Jong... Hmm.

His first missions were simple, taking money and ration coupons to people in hiding.

Gasp, gasp... There's not much chance of running into the Germans on such a miserable day...

Later the missions were more dangerous... weapon drops...

Hurry! I hear a car coming. Let's go!

Good, precisely as planned...

...the robbery of a distribution center.

If you just stay calm, you'll be fine!

Enough ration coupons for hundreds in hiding.

The Nazis crushed the Resistance using any means.

Quite a good catch today!

We tortured that prisoner until he told us their names...

Many members of the Resistance were executed by the Nazis...

FIRE!

Long live the Queen!

May you burn in Hell!

There were also those Dutch who helped the Germans, and made lots of money...

They want more bunkers from us, in case of an invasion...

Fine! We'll be rich!

Others, black marketeers, profited from the shortages.

Cigarettes and Dutch gin... 400 guilders.*

You're a crook!

Let's buy the stuff anyway...

*Today around U.S. $250

And there was always that threat of being betrayed by a snitch.

There are people hiding at No. 8 Kerkstraat...

Most of the Dutch just tried to go about their normal lives...

HET VERLEDEN
GRANDIOSE SUCCESFILM met ZARAH LEANDER

ZARAH LEANDER   HANS STOWE

Luckily, we can still go to the movies!

To forget the war for a moment...

Many thought about their own needs first...

The man from No. 15 was arrested!

His own fault.

It's best to just mind your own business...

BAKKER

I was so lonesome during the winter of 1943–44...

Esther's gone, delivered to the Germans by my own father... My brothers are gone...

I hardly saw my father. He usually worked the night shift to avoid quarrelling with my mother...

Helena, please go and see if the grocery store has kerosene for the lamp. Shut the door quietly...

Sigh! Yes, Mother... I know, Father is sleeping.

I just hope there isn't a long line...

There she is!

That was quick! Mother will be happy with the kerosene.

KRUIDENIE

WINTERHULP
○ wij geven
○ 5% van onze
○ winst

It feels as if I'm being followed!

Oh no! Another razzia!

Run, it's the Krauts!

RIVOLI
ufa Film
MARIKA RÖKK
KASSA

Awful! To have to go to Germany...

Pick up all the men between 18 and 50!

Forced labor...

PTT

Where did that guy go?

Helena van Dort?

OH!

?!?

Sorry, I didn't mean to scare you. Wim sent me...

Wim... my brother Wim? I... How is...?

He's doing just fine and said I could ask you to help us...

Help? How can I help?

We need somebody who's prepared to act as a courier. It's important and your brother said—

—that I would help out... It's true!

I distributed underground newspapers that were printed in a basement.

Keep going with that stinking fish!

VISHANDEL KOLK

Pfff... That was a close call... If he only had a clue...

My father handed over our radio when he had to. My new friends had cleverly hidden their radio...

Umph!... Let's see what Radio Orange has to report!

They should really make smaller radios...

People of western Europe, a landing was made this morning on the coast of France...

The invasion! Finally!

1944 6 juni

...Together with our Russian allies, we're going to liberate Europe...

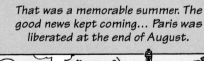

That was a memorable summer. The good news kept coming... Paris was liberated at the end of August.

Paris has been liberated! Hitler's order to destroy the city was ignored by the German general in command there.

And then, on September 4, 1944...

Helena! Hurry! You won't believe your ears.

Radio Orange reporting. The Allied forces have crossed into the Netherlands.

Unbelievable! It's going so well...

Finally! The Liberation...

The next day, the wildest rumors were flying...

The Brits have crossed our southern border!

Americans have been sighted close by! We have to hurry to the city line! Our liberators will soon be in Amsterdam!

Where are they all going?

To Germany! The rats are deserting the sinking ship!

Of course they are, those Nazi collaborators!*

*People who helped the German Occupier

We got excited too soon. The Nazis still controlled Amsterdam. That day was later called Dolle Dinsdag ("Crazy Tuesday"). However, the south of the Netherlands was liberated.

We'll cross the Rhine at Arnhem...

Once we've crossed over, Holland will be liberated and then we'll advance into Germany...

A huge Allied assault of the most important bridges by Arnhem and Nijmegen took place on September 17, 1944...

Hello, I'm Wim de Jong. I'm carrying vital information from the Resistance.

Jolly good, old boy. Why is the German opposition here so strong?

It's a big armored division...

Is that so? Then we should ask HQ* for help.

*Headquarters

The assault failed...

We have to retreat. Join us if you like...

Eh... yes... sure!

The Dutch government exiled in London called for a railway strike to hinder the Occupier, so hardly any food could be delivered by train...

Life is going to get even worse...

Alles nu op de bon

Yes, now we have to stand in line for everything!

I'm afraid these rations are even less than we had before...

I'm so hungry!

The winter of 1944–45 became known as the Hunger Winter.

Quickly! Hide the bread under your coat.

Hurry! The Germans are coming!

Give it... umph!

I can hear their dogs barking.

BAKKERIJ

STEHEN BLEIBEN!! HALT!!

What do you have there, boy?!

𝔚𝔬𝔬𝔣! 𝔚𝔬𝔬𝔣! 𝔚𝔬𝔬𝔣!

There were many razzias. Fifty thousand men and boys were transported from Rotterdam. They were put to work shoring up the German line of defense.

I don't care if each and every one of you drops dead digging. As long as I get my anti-tank ditch!

Coal was scarce...

Luckily we still have that old woodstove. It's good for burning everything.

Now if we just had something to cook on it... What a shame...

Wood for burning was gathered up from everywhere. Empty houses were stripped...

Take care! A house like that collapsed!

Hey, what would the people who lived here think of this mess?

They were Jews...

Mother, stop, otherwise the sack will be too heavy.

But that wood from between the rails burns so well!

One morning in January 1945...

Mother! I've been asked to take a group of children to Friesland. If they stay here they'll starve, but farmers there still have some food.

Gulp...

I was going to stay there too.

Please write!

I hope they'll be okay...

Oh, the Red Cross... They're not a target!

x

47

Soup kitchens where people could get something to eat opened in the west of the country.

What is this anyway? It looks like glue!

It's stew.

Look how hungry they are...

Poor things...

VOLKS GAARKEUKE

My mother wrote and told me that she and a neighbor had started going outside the city to try to find food.

We can put a lot in this baby carriage.

I hope they still have some food left for us...

My mother and her neighbor were not the only ones who set off on such journeys...

I'm afraid that some people will never make it home...

What choice do they have? Dying of starvation?

Can't you give me some more potatoes for this necklace? It's a family heirloom.

No, then we won't have any for ourselves.

The journeys were hard... the disappointments many.

We're almost home... Oh no!

The Landwacht!*

*Auxiliary police composed of Dutch Nazis

At least we didn't confiscate everything...

Animals!

More than 20,000 people died of hunger and cold that winter... When we were utterly desperate, food fell from the sky...

That British plane is coming in very low...

The Germans are allowing it. Their anti-aircraft gunners won't shoot them down.

48

The food shortages in Friesland weren't so bad, but we were still happy when the spring of 1945 arrived...

Thanks for letting me stay until the Liberation...

It won't be long now...

I just heard the latest news report...

Hitler is now completely surrounded by the Allies...

Once the Brits and Americans advance from the west and join the Russians from the east, the war will be over...

SCHOOL PLAAT 1928

Berlijn

Hitler is trapped...

Friesland was liberated on April 15, 1945...

Now it is really almost over! The Germans are withdrawing!

...On May 5, 1945, we finally heard the news that we had been waiting for...

The German Army has surrendered...

We're finally free!

The war is over!

In the middle of the festivities, my Friesian father arrived with bad news.

?!?

Helena! Something's happened in Amsterdam.

Yesterday, German soldiers opened fire on the crowd celebrating downtown. Many people were killed or wounded...

Fire! That'll teach them to celebrate!

RATATATATA

Perhaps my mother has been hurt... or my father...

I need to go to Amsterdam!

Of course!

The next day...

You can hitch a ride on this BS* truck all the way to Alkmaar.

Thanks for everything!

I want to go home too!

You have to stay a bit longer...

*Dutch Forces of the Interior

49

Thanks, boys!

Sigh... Ah, to be young again!

Gulp... I hope everything is okay...

What a mess! This is not like my mother...

I thought I heard something. I'm so glad you're back, Helena!

Hello! Is everything okay? Have you seen my mother?

She's staying with your aunt Bep and is fine, but your father...

I must go to her right away!

Oh, the neighbor wanted to tell me about my father...

...I wonder what's happened to him?

Those who collaborated should be dealt with!

Yes, they should be severely punished!

Gulp...

Luckily, Aunt Bep and my mother were at home...

Oh, my dear child. I'm so glad that you're back!

Oh, Mother, it's so good to see you too! But... what's happened to Father? Where is he?!

Oh, Helena! They came and got Father...

The BS arrested everyone they suspected of collaborating with the Germans...

Let's go, you traitor!

You're mistaken!

ORAN

We'll see about that later!

They have locked them up in the storehouses in the harbor. It's so terrible!

Don't you dare complain. Because otherwise...

DOKEN VERBODEN

How humiliating...

A week later...

Hello, Aunt Bep! Are Mother and Helena here?

Of course! Come right on in!

Helena!

Oh, Wim!

Oh, my boy, I have been so worried!

I enlisted with an English Army unit. I also met up with the Russian fighting troops...

Hey, English! You drink vodka?!

I'm from Holland! Got any ol' Dutch gin?

...The Russians told us the most awful stories. They liberated camps in Poland that the Nazis built especially to kill as many people as possible... and in particular the Jews of Europe...

So they were murdered with this gas?

They thought they were going to shower and...

Did the Nazis tattoo those numbers on your arms?

Yes, on the arms of all the people who could work. Children and the elderly were killed when they arrived...

Most prisoners died from exhaustion or were murdered in the gas chambers. As were thousands of Jews from the Netherlands.

Oh, Esther! She must be dead.

Good gracious!

The survivors of the camps began returning. For a while, I went to the Central Train Station every day...

Did you know Esther Hecht?

No.

Sob... It's hopeless... Nobody's seen her...

Some more very sad news arrived...

This letter was just delivered...

What is it, Mother?

...due to an unfortunate accident, your husband has died in prison.

A week later I was standing beside my father's grave...

Oh, why did he collaborate with the Germans?

The war in Asia didn't end until August 15, 1945. Japan surrendered after two atom bombs were dropped on Hiroshima and Nagasaki. We were very worried about Aunt Riek...

It's a letter from Uncle Cor...

Please read it aloud, Mother.

Terrible things were done to them...

Europeans were imprisoned in camps. And the men were separated from the women and the children.

Cor thought he would never see Riek and André again...

Farewell, dears!

I love you, Cor!

Papa!

The prisoners in the camp had to pay their daily respects to the Japanese Emperor Hirohito.

Bow, lower, lower...!

The camp guards handed out cruel punishments.

15 lashes is enough...

That'll teach them!

Pens and writing paper are forbidden...

When boys turned 12, they were transferred to one of the men's camps...

Be brave, son!

Sob... Will I ever see him again?

The men were often forced to carry out heavy labor...

I can't handle this anymore, Cor...

C'mon!

急いで!*

*Hurry up!

Many prisoners died of disease and malnutrition.

Give this to my wife...

Of course...

Some no longer believed they would survive. Still, others tried to keep everybody's spirits up...

...The Japanese are going to lose the war...

...It won't be long now...

I wonder how Riek and André are?

Uncle Cor described the Liberation.

Look! It's American! The first one in three years!

Unbelievable!

One morning, at the end of August...

What's happened?

Where did all the Japs go?

Major De Wildt wants to speak...

The Japanese Emperor has decided to stop fighting... We're free!

They have lost the war!

Now everything will return to normal...

People were celebrating outside the camp as well... but for very different reasons!

MERDEKA!* We're not your colony anymore!

We are now a free republic.

What kind of nonsense is this?

*Freedom!

I just want to go back to my plantation...

This plantation is now ours!

Let's go, before they kill us!

The camp was the safest place...

We'll be okay here.

Of course we will. The Japanese have orders from the English to protect us...

MERDEKA!

But some of the Japanese gave weapons to the rebellious Indonesians.

Yes! This will come in very handy!

Now we're in control!

A British Army battalion finally reached the camp where Riek, Cor and André had been reunited...

...I'm handing over this camp to you...

Listen... your men have orders to protect the people in this camp.

The Dutch living here must be taken to a safe area of the island.

Hai!

That's how the Japanese ended up helping the English...

This route is too dangerous. The rebels have rifles and even machine guns!

Gulp... Is that so?

An ambush!

Argh, Mother... I've been hit!

Not all the liberated prisoners reached the coast safely.

Riek, not you too! Don't leave me!

Survived three years in a camp to die anyway...

...sob... My sister... My nephew

Oh, I'm so sorry, Mother... but luckily you still have us!

We did not know what to do next...

How will we go on?

In the spring of 1946, my mother came to a decision.

So many horrible things have happened here...

I want to go back to my hometown...

Sounds like a good plan!

Count me in...

A month later, the moving truck was on our doorstep.

It's better that they're leaving...

Everybody here knows her husband collaborated with the Germans.

He even took part in razzias in his own neighborhood.

I hope we can now put the war behind us, Helena.

I wonder...

What should we do with Father's uniform?

Dear me, such devastation!

...But look how hard they're working!

Hello, I'm your neighbor from No. 47. Do you need a hand?

She's a war widow from the big city.

Yes, all those poor victims of the Hunger Winter.

So they never found out that your father—

—had helped the Germans? No! Thank goodness.

Then what happened? Did your mother remarry? And what happened to Wim?

My mother never really recovered from the war. She died in 1954...

Things would have been different without that terrible war...

Perhaps, but we'll never know...

Then a few years after Mom died, I met your grandfather...

Uh... Helena... would you like to dance?

Hee hee... I thought you'd never ask, Kees.

We married soon after. It was the time of the postwar reconstruction and we didn't have much money.

Go easy with the rice! During the war it was worth a fortune!

To the happy couple!!!

Wim emigrated to Canada...

I hope he'll write.

Oh, now I'm all alone!

You have me, sweetheart!

We lived in my mother's house for a short while, but...

If our house is ready on time, then the little one will be born there.

Your father was born there in 1962, Jeroen...

I miss my family... and Esther...

I often thought about Esther... especially each year on our Memorial Day, May 4.

Now, two minutes of silence to remember the victims of the war...

1940 1945

Look at the time! You'd better hurry home, Jeroen, or your mother will be angry with me!

Call and say I'm on my way...

Your kris...

...Now I'm going to get it!

Why are you so late, Jeroen?!

Sorry! Gran was telling me about the war.

Yes, he just walked in...

Every year she dragged me to the ceremony to commemorate the dead. So I'd watch out!

But she never talks about the war...

And what about things to sell on Queen's Day?

I completely forgot... She let me have this dagger, but I won't sell it! Tomorrow I'll go by her house again.

Queen's Day is great. I finally found all the back issues of my favorite fishing magazine...

On May 4...

Gran didn't sound good on the phone...

Gran, Mom lent me your key! What's the matter? Are you okay?

Oh, sweet boy! I sprained my ankle and can't walk at all!

Now I can't go to the Memorial Day service.

58

I'll go for you!

Gasp... I hope I'm not too late...

I've lived in the United States for more than fifty years. But during the war I was hidden in a village nearby...

Phew... Just in time...

I survived the persecution of the Jews...

My friend Helena, who wasn't Jewish, was a great comfort to me.

Huh?

Thank you, Mrs. Leibowitz, for that moving story! And now for the traditional two minutes of silence...

Impossible! But...

Could it be?

Mind if I ask you something?

Of course not...

Is Leibowitz your married name?

60

When I came home from school that day, your father was waiting for me...

Hello, what's wrong?

Just come with me!

He wanted to help me!

I have strict orders to deliver this Jewess where she belongs!

Yes, sir!

I gave him the address of a dear friend of my parents and he took me there immediately.

I will say that I couldn't find her after school.

Esther! Come inside quickly!

What! My father saved you? He never said anything.

Oh, Esther, we have so much to catch up on...

Uh-oh. I'm outta here, once is enough...

Bye... I gotta be home on time!

A *Family Secret* was originally published in Dutch in 2007 by the Anne Frank House in cooperation with the Resistance Museum of Friesland under the title *De Ontdekking*

This edition is published in agreement with the Anne Frank House

This edition published 2011 by Macmillan Children's Books
a division of Macmillan Publishers Limited
20 New Wharf Road, London N1 9RR
Basingstoke and Oxford
Associated companies throughout the world
www.panmacmillan.com

ISBN 978-0-330-51982-3

Drawings
Eric Heuvel
Scenario
Eric Heuvel
Menno Metselaar (Anne Frank House)
Ruud van der Rol
Hans Groeneweg (Resistance Museum of Friesland)
English Translation
Lorraine T. Miller (Epicycles, Amsterdam)
Creative Process Support
Ruud de Grefte
Coloring
Hanneke Bons
Research and Documentation
Jacqueline Koerts
Design
Karel Oosting, Amsterdam
Production
Anne Frank House, Amsterdam

A FAMILY SECRET was originally published in Dutch as DE ONTDEKKING, thanks in part to funding provided by the Ministry of Public Health, Welfare and Sport (VWS) in the Netherlands.

We are thankful to the many people who offered their commentary and advice in the planning and creation of this graphic novel:
Liesbeth van der Horst (Dutch Resistance Museum, Amsterdam)
Hetty Berg (Stichting Het Indisch Huis, The Hague)

Annemiek Gringold and Petra Katzenstein (Jewish Historical Museum, Amsterdam)
Dirk Mulder (Memorial Center Camp Westerbork)
Nine Nooter (National Committee May 4th and 5th)
Erik Somers (Netherlands Institute for War Documentation / NIOD)
Stef Temming (National War and Resistance Museum, Overloon)
Christel Tijenk (National Museum Zuid-Holland, Gouda)
Jan-Durk Tuinier and Geu Visser (Memorial Center Fort de Bilt, Utrecht)
Mieke Sobering (Anne Frank House)
Tom van der Geugten (Fontys Secondary Teacher Training College, Tilburg)
VMBO (Vocational High School) Teachers (and students)
Wim Borghuis and Hans Werker (CSG De Goudse Waarden, Gouda)
Henk Botter (Wellantcollege, Alphen aan de Rijn)
Anke van den Tempel (Montessori College Oost, Amsterdam)
Adult Education Teachers
Chris van Asperen (ROC Rijn Ijssel College Arnhem)
Merel Borgesius (ROC of Amsterdam)
Primary School Teachers
Sijmen Sijtsma and Lolkje Algra (Prof. Grewelschool, Leeuwarden)
Matty Delgrosso (OBS Grou, Grou)
Daniëlle Dijkmeijer (Prins Constantijnschool PCBO, Leeuwarden)
Jan Veltman and Jeanne Minks (Albertine Agnesschool PCBO, Leeuwarden)